I Love You As Much

Mari Loder

Illustrations by Katy England

Katy England

Mari Loder

ISBN 978-1-64028-046-5 (Paperback)
ISBN 978-1-64028-047-2 (Digital)

Christian Faith Publishing, Inc.
296 Chestnut Street
Meadville, PA 16335
www.christianfaithpublishing.com

Printed in the United States of America

I Love You As Much

Mari Loder

Illustrations by Katy England

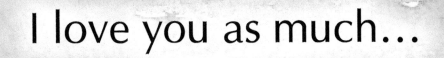

I love you as much...

As the ocean is blue.

I love you as much…

As the Bible is true.

I love you as much…

As the sun is bright.

I love you as much…

As a clear, starry night.

I love you as much...

As the flowers bloom and grow.

I love you as much…

As God loves you, you know.

I love you as much…

13

As the stars in the sky.

I love you as much…

As the mountains are high.

16

I love you as much...

As the wind and the rain.

I love you as much…

As the sweeping Kansas plain.

I love you as much…

21

As the first fallen snow.

I love you as much…

As the green valleys below.

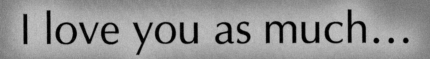

I love you as much…

As the heavens above.

I love you as much...

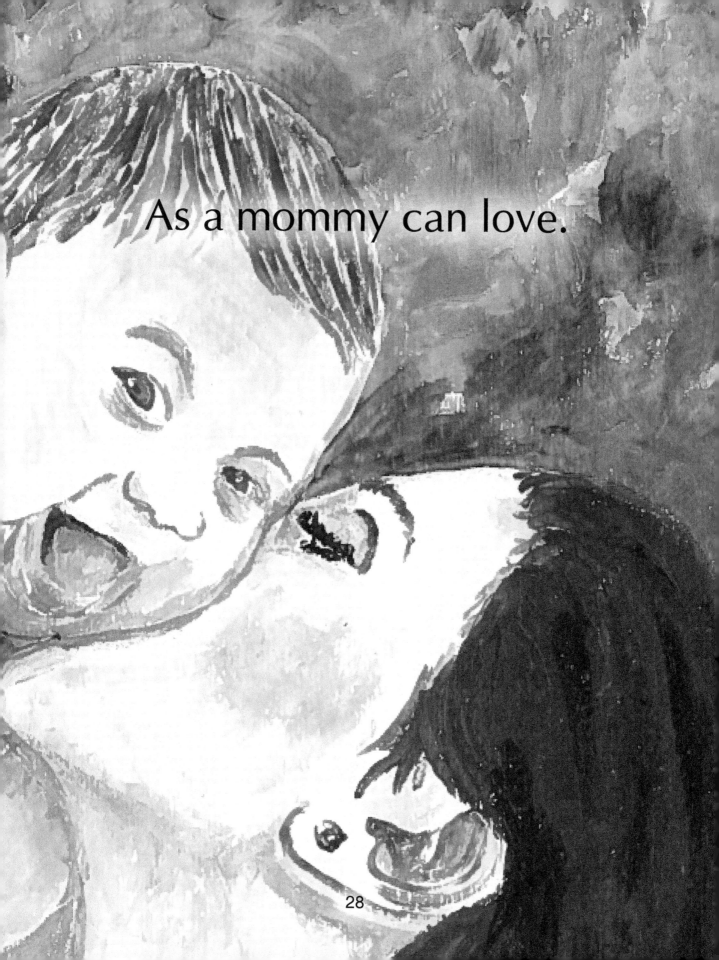

As a mommy can love.

About the Author

A former teacher, Mari has a passion for reading and for children's literature that she has passed on to her children. A mother of four, Mari has had an interest in publishing her own book since 1993. Now that she is an empty nester, it is finally happening! She has a passion for life lessons and faith-based teachings for children. Mari's sister, Katy England, created all the illustrations, fulfilling a dream that both have fostered together.

CPSIA information can be obtained
at www.ICGtesting.com
Printed in the USA
LVOW05s2339021117
554653LV00002B/2/P